# Be a good leader

How to be a good leader and gaining the heart of those you a leading

Raymond H.boyd

# Table of contents

1.

2.
3.
4.
5.


## Chapter 1

Abilities of a decent leader
There is no one-of-a-kind
method for depicting
incredible leadership abilities.
Leadership abilities are the
capacities individuals need to
lead and convey projects,
support drives, construct a
feeling of normal reason, and
enable others.
Leadership abilities
additionally incorporate the
capacities individuals need to
control workers toward the
accomplishment of the
business objectives, move
them, drive change, and
convey results.
Consistent with saying certain
individuals are normal leaders
however it is likewise a fact
that leadership can be
learned.
Objective Setting
The capacity to lay out
objectives is one of the central

abilities of a compelling leader. Objectives provide you a feeling of guidance yet the advantages head a lot farther than knowing how to coordinate your group. As a leader, objectives offer the response regarding what to do straightaway, permits you to survey your group's exhibition against concurred targets and KPIs, and empower you to expand your own and your laborer's proficiency.

Assignment

No obvious leader demands keeping up with all control, everything being equal. That approach is counterproductive and contradicts the meaning of a leader. The best leaders have become amazing at the designation. Doing so appropriately implies that you are engaging and fostering your kin and cultivating a cooperative workplace, which is all quality of extraordinary leadership.

Independent direction

The capacity to settle on a choice is frequently viewed as

the foundation of successful leadership. As a leader, those working under you and those above you who have requested that you further develop the association's main concern trust you to assume responsibility and go with significant choices. You may not necessarily in every case pursue the ideal choice but rather conciseness makes one in any case; a leader can constantly choose to follow an alternate way.

Correspondence

Turning into a powerful leader without first turning into an extraordinary communicator is unthinkable. That doesn't mean excelling at talking; a great many people can do this entirely well. A leader will offer respectability and genuineness when they talk however, more critically, they will know when to tune in. They will figure out that lucidity - being explicit rather than equivocal - will further develop their relational abilities, as well working on

their capacity to peruse
between the so-called lines.
Using time productively
From dealing with a group to
searching for new deals and
promoting potential open
doors and getting new sellers,
leaders frequently end up
turning many plates. If you
neglect to deal with your time
successfully, those plates will
before long come crashing
down, so it is not difficult to
see the reason why using
time effectively is the center
expertise of in leadership. By
utilizing your time, you will
probably motivate your group
to do likewise.
Critical thinking
Your capacity to take care of
issues will fundamentally
affect your prosperity as a
leader. While you should
allow your group to take care
of their concerns, the buck
commonly stops with you.
Most issues can be settled by
applying a basic four-step
approach: characterizing the
issue, distinguishing likely
arrangements, assessing and
choosing from the potential

arrangements, and carrying out your picked approach. Relationship Building Leaders should have the capacity to support associations with workers, key providers and clients, and friends. As you ascend the leadership stepping stool, this rundown might extend to incorporate partners, funders, the media, and exchange bodies. In this regard, leadership can be seen as the result of a few connections. At the point when you fabricate significant associations with others, you are much better positioned to work together.

Key reasoning and acting Organizations today should stay agile and receptive to change, which is the reason key reasoning is among the most profoundly viable leaders. A vital way to deal with leadership was multiple times more essential to the view of adequacy than different ways of behaving it examined, remembering correspondence and hands-for strategic ways of behaving. Key masterminds take a wide, long-range way to deal with critical thinking and dynamic that includes objective investigation, thinking ahead, and arranging.

"Leaders need to contemplate the best course to get to the results that surpass the assumptions of individuals they serve. "There are numerous approaches to that, including setting a dream and being clear about what that implies, alongside everybody's part in accomplishing that vision."

Development

For organizations to keep pace in the present serious commercial center, advancement should be an authoritative need — and this kind of culture begins at the top. It's simple for leaders to become trapped in an endless cycle of playing out their regular obligations since individuals are predictable animals, Bullock says. Development is a decent way for leaders to switch things around and take a stab at a genuinely new thing — which at times prompts good thoughts and better strategies.

"Leaders need to establish a climate where individuals have a good sense of security to take a stab at a novel, new thing, find out how it turns out, and even fizzle," he says. "In the present speedy world, individuals are hesitant to attempt new things."

Yet again this begins by setting the model yourself. It's pleasant to suggest that leaders make time consistently to have a go at a genuinely new thing, whether it's another cycle or idea."Leadership is inseparable from learning,".

"The best leaders are the ones who are continually learning and sorting out some way to fill the holes and foster abilities that are the most significant to them."

Compassion is related to work execution and is a basic piece of the capacity to understand people at their core and

leadership viability. If you
show more comprehensive
leadership and sympathetic
ways of behaving toward your
immediate reports, our
exploration demonstrates
you're bound to be seen as a
superior entertainer by your
chief. Additionally,
compassion and
consideration are goals for
further developing work
environment conditions for
people around you.
Learning deftness is the
capacity to understand what
to do when you don't have the
foggiest idea of what to do.
On the off chance that you're
a "fast review" or can succeed
in new conditions, you could
as of now be learning lithe. In
any case, anyone can
encourage learning readiness
through training, experience,
and exertion. Investigate how
extraordinary leaders are
incredible students with solid
learning deftness to get
everything rolling.
Regard
Approaching individuals with
deference consistently is quite

possibly the main thing a leader can do. It will ease pressures and struggle, make trust, and further develop viability. Regard is about more than the shortfall of disregard, and it very well may be displayed in various ways. Investigate how you can develop an environment of regard at work or more deeply study ways that you can turn into a partner to other people.

Appreciation

Being appreciative can prompt higher confidence, diminished sadness and tension, and better rest. Appreciation could make you a superior leader. However, a couple of individuals routinely say "much obliged" in work settings, even though the vast majority say they'd turn out more diligently for a grateful chief. The best leaders know how to exhibit genuine appreciation in the work environment.

Chapter 2

Step-by-step instructions to further develop leadership abilities

Figure out Your Style of Leadership

To work on your expertise, you want to have a cutlass-like comprehension of how you manifest that ability in the work environment. Your style of leadership alludes to the ways by which you direct your group, keep them roused and execute your arrangements. No two leaders have precisely the same style and understanding, yours will take a considerable lot of self-reflection and contribution from outside parties. You want to understand what your commonplace disposition resembles at work, how much acclaim you give versus the number of evaluates you normally offer, and how open you are with your group, from there, the sky is the limit. Doing this assists you with figuring out what your assets are and where improvement is required.

Reinforce Your Shortcomings

Having perceived your way of driving, the subsequent stage you need to take is to refine the shortcomings you recognized in the past step. For example, you might be perfect at making plans yet have difficulties dealing with the group to finish them effectively. Or on the other hand, you may be capable of addressing the group collectively yet battle with composing interchanges. Anything that the shortcoming, you can peruse supportive material or take online courses in leadership to assist you with turning into a vastly improved leader.

Improve as a Communicator Somehow or another, leadership is a ceaseless series of discussions between the leader and the group. On the off chance that you can't convey as expected, conciseness wants to steer your group where it needs to head. Do you have great report composing abilities however find it hard to stand up during group gatherings? Or then again do you do well in private discussions yet find it trying to send a fitting email? This is certainly one hole that you want to quickly right. Luckily, there are heaps of courses in correspondence that you can enroll in immediately.

Put forth Clear Objectives and Work Towards Them

To become effective as a leader, you should have an objective that you have situated your group towards and effectively conquer chances to accomplish. Pick a beneficial objective for your group to focus on and devise a strong game plan that your group will execute to meet the objective. Set significant benchmarks so you can continuously register to be certain that you are gaining satisfactory headway and can address any mistakes that happen as fast as could be expected. Make a strategy for attaching new difficulties so you can lessen the interaction to a repeatable framework. Whenever you have arrived at an objective, focus on another, ceaselessly pushing forward to accomplish significant objectives that will give you and your representatives deep satisfaction.

Get Better at Simply deciding

Any group pursuing an objective will experience spots in the excursion where choices should be made. For these, they will typically focus on the group leader - you. As a leader, you will find that navigation is a weight that should be conveyed appropriately and that the expense of settling on unfortunate choices is high. Your capacity to settle on great quality choices under extreme conditions should continually be honed to guide your group on the right course and keep away from business disasters ahead.

Acknowledge Disappointments and Gain From Them

Regardless of how talented you become as a leader, you won't ever be safe from committing errors. Be that as it may, a genuine leader isn't anxious about committing

errors. They perceive their blunders and discuss them transparently. They gain from those mix-ups and work to gather them. They will tell their colleagues, "I committed this error and it caused this impact. How might I abstain from rehashing this misstep, going ahead?" Having the option to open up and gain from your mix-ups passes a strong message on to your group; it lets them know that you are a leader that can continually improve and urges them to do likewise. For you to acknowledge disappointments, you should recognize the spots where you are powerless and need improvement. This capacity to appropriately recognize your shortcomings as a leader is enough canvassed in one of the passages above.
Resolve clashes
Try not to be chief from damnation! Not every person will get along constantly. Rather than overlooking relational struggles and trusting they will disappear,

address them by conversing
with those included secretly.
Additionally, be available to
reassign colleagues on the off
chance that the contention
can't be settled.
Create situational mindfulness
A characteristic of a decent
leader is somebody who can
see the master plan and
expect issues before they
happen. This is significant
expertise to have while taking
care of perplexing ventures
with tight cutoff times. The
capacity to predict and give
ideas to keep away from
potential issues is important
for a leader. This capacity
additionally assists you with
perceiving open doors that
others neglect, which will
surely procure you
acknowledgment. This can be
particularly challenging to
create while driving remote
groups yet with training, you
can turn out to be more
receptive to your groups and
tasks.
Leadership expertise is
something that can be learned
and isn't an ability that one

should be brought into the
world with. On the off chance
that you will evaluate yourself,
work on your shortcomings,
and figure out how to convey
and go with better choices,
you will end up being a more
talented leader.


Chapter 3

Techniques of a decent leader
Try not to attempt to force
yourself
You shouldn't feel that driving
through the force of a position
is a decent technique. A tyrant
director winds up deterring
and subverting their group's
advancement potential.
 Increment your insight
(consistently)
Fundamentally, a leader is
continuously searching for
ways of further developing
their leadership skills.
Whether by taking courses,
understanding books, going to
talks, or imparting encounters
to different experts. Try to
oftentimes move along.
Know your group

To lead, it is basic to know who you are driving. In this way, look to comprehend the particularities and necessities of every individual in your team. Only then will it be feasible to make a superior relationship with them, as well as how to propel them and concentrate from every single one of them their best potential.

Adaptability

Try not to attempt to restrict yourself to incredibly severe principles. Comprehend that changes are normal and that keeping an extremely safe position might slow advance.

Concede your mix-ups

Have you committed an error? Just let it out and address it. A decent leader never evades liabilities and should be modest in perceiving any errors.

Know how to tune in

It is essential to comprehend that a leadership position doesn't imply that subordinate suppositions ought not to be heard.

In this way, pay attention to
your group! Numerous smart
thoughts can arise and be
incredible learning
experiences. Have the option
to acknowledge ideas.
Furthermore, the innovative
capability of workers can
increment as well as their
feeling of inspiration.
Center around individuals
As well as knowing subtleties
and paying attention to your
group, a leader genuinely
must never truly lose contact
with their teammates. Live
day to day and forever be
ready, all things considered, it
is significant to know the
proper behavior in a
preventive and oversee
chances.
Also, will always remember:
you're driving individuals!
Accordingly, perceive the
breaking point that isolates
proficient life from staff.
Be the model
Do you require dependability?
Be on time, for instance,
motivate those you lead, and
gain their trust.
 Act with balance

Attempt to continuously keep up with balance and the capacity to appreciate anyone on a deeper level, as well as not to misrepresent comparable to individuals you lead. Too many prizes, inordinate punishments, or leaning toward certain workers are perspectives that ought to be kept away from.
Know how to define objectives It is no utilization specifying objectives that can not be accomplished - aside from not finding success, it will just establish an upsetting and useless climate.
Know your business, your group, and your expertise to put forth feasible objectives.
Try not to disclose reactions Issues with a giver? Keep away from analysis in broad daylight. Talk straightforwardly to the worker and make the important evaluations and reactions in private.
 Figure out the market
To know how to lead well, it is fundamental to profoundly comprehend the market

where your organization operates. Always keep awake to date with data about financial variables, contenders, and clients. Furthermore, showing better direction will give your group more noteworthy security. Support interest and collaboration
By empowering the support of your representatives, you make a more dynamic, drew-in, and thusly roused group. The produced learning will likewise be fundamental for the additional expert improvement of every colleague. Furthermore, fostering collaboration abilities, all things considered, more noteworthy incorporation between representatives will increment efficiency.
 Regard for criticism
Input is crucial for keeping up with great individuals on the board: you can address disappointments or commendations of the outcome of each employee. Give criticism through

individual discussions and consistently consider substantial information to demonstrate your evaluation. Perceive your representatives Have you seen an uplifting outlook? Perceive your representatives! All things considered, group inspiration is a definitive figure of efficiency. Observe the inward guidelines laid out by the organization and set up as a regular occurrence motivator lobbies for good outcomes.
 Hierarchical Environment Studies
To know how to lead is to know how to investigate the environment of your group. To do this, utilization overviews with polls that can demonstrate the degree of representative fulfillment and engagement. Take the outcomes truly and give the required changes distinguished in the reactions to further develop worker commitment.
Know how to impart
Knowing how to convey is fundamental. It merits

planning gatherings with the group and in any event, utilizing innovation to further develop discourse and the trading of data.

Try not to delay independent direction

Try not to put off simply deciding - regardless of whether the issues include some intricacy.

A decent leader should know their situation, generally, a sensation of uncertainty and hesitation is given to the group.

Deal with key preparation

To use wise judgment and fabricate objectives that guide the exercises of your representatives, it is basic to know how to design them.

To do this, utilization methods, programming, and key arranging apparatuses in your organization.

Grasp a bunch of assumptions for you

Comprehend the assumptions your group has about your leadership.

Do they anticipate more successive and clear input?

Open doors for preparing?
More gatherings?
Conversing with your
representatives can assist you
with understanding where you
are going wrong.
 Try not to take on obligations
that have been appointed to
another person
Try not to take on tasks that
you have designated for
another person. Figure out
how to deal with the
circumstance in any event,
when the outcomes are not
putting on a show of being
normal.
Converse with the worker, be
honest and help in what is
essential, however, don't take
on someone else's obligation.
Have a feeling of need
What is the most critical
undertaking? Figure out how
to order exercises
corresponding to need. The
whole group must know what
to do first.
Figure out how to design
ahead of time
Try not to assign undertakings
just before they're expected -
as well as creating

uneasiness in the group, almost certainly, the nature of the outcome won't be perfect. To do this, figure out how to coordinate exercises and represent them ahead of time. Train the group and recognize the ability

A decent leader is a proficient who looks to prepare their workers, intending to continuously work on the organization - and unafraid of interior rivalry.

Likewise, look out for skilled individuals in your group. Remember them and put resources into their turn of events.

It isn't sufficient to just utilize great leadership strategies and methods, think long haul, and about the efficiency of your organization.

Be a decent leader: make new leaders for what's in store!


Chapter 4

The most effective method to Improve as a Leader

Great leaders have their work completely under control. In any case, most have needed to buckle down on themselves — by overseeing or company-satiating for possible vocation restricting qualities. To develop as a leader, you want to perceive and deal with your most grounded inclinations Raymond pictures when pictures chiefs recognize a leader they respect, they frequently underrate how much that individual might have battled to check specific examples of conduct or certain predominant features of their character. Extraordinary leaders have it under control. Yet, in truth, the most successful leaders that we have noticed. The characteristics that work well for a chief in one leadership position frequently don't function admirably in another. Climbing the progressive system into new jobs or conditions, chiefs might find they need to play up or get control over various features of their entity. What qualities can become shortcomings? Luckily, propels in character exploration can furnish leaders with a lot more extravagant image of their character. Analysts have recognized incalculable attributes that recognize people from each other. Research in late many years has con-came close to five wide aspects, each containing a bunch of characteristics. These aspects show up so powerful that they have been named the Enormous Five. Now generally acknowledged, a similar five fac-pinnacles are found reliably with various exploration techniques, as well as across time, settings and cultures. To stand out from different models of character, the Huge Five were gotten from the ordinary language that individuals use to portray each other. Beginning with an expert rundown of almost 18,000 men quality descriptors, the rundown was ultimately reduced to five crucial elements: the need for stability, extraversion, transparency, pleasantness, and scruples.

Character scores are not execution scores; no character qualities lead straightforwardly to positive or negative execution. Notwithstanding, those scores can make chiefs aware of regions that require consideration. A quality that is successful in one setting might become redundant or counterproductive when the circumstance changes.

 Need for Solidness: The amount of Pressure Is Too Much? Emotional steadiness can be an important quality for executives, assisting them with adapting to pressure, misfortunes, and vulnerability. Yet, it has its disadvantages, as well.

You can be excessively formed. Balance under tension assists chiefs with projecting a consoling picture when others might be leaned to overreact. Numerous leaders, we mentor value their capacity to try to avoid panicking. The gamble of this quality is that they can seem unacceptable or ailing in desperation. They might experience issues understanding the reason why others are concerned. In addition, such leaders might appear to be unduly sure. One technique to counter overoptimism is to make mental records. Close by three confident purposes behind why something will work out, a chief inclined to over-optimism ought to think of three bleak justifications for why it may not. Or on the other hand, you can be excessively fretful — and go overboard. Some of the time effective chiefs have an articulated propensity to be eager. Robert Iger, Chief of Walt Disney, has recognized in an article in the New York Times that this is a region he's dealt with: "I've learned, as a rule, to be quieter. … I've figured out how to listen better and oversee response time better. What I mean by that isn't blowing up to things that are shared with me, because occasionally it's not difficult to do that." Certain chiefs we mentor are less versatile to stress and battle to keep cool-headed, mirroring a significant requirement for strength. Again and again, they manage their annoyance by stifling it. The issue is that the displeasure can ac-cumulate concealed and unexpressed until it gushes out over on a clueless casualty. To abstain from going overboard, executives need to find approaches to discharging their annoyance holder before it arrives at the edge. The easiest technique is to express those pessimistic feelings: "I feel disheartened/baffled/upset/bothered because... ."

Exploration in cerebrum imaging recommends that articulating our sentiments hoses those sentiments. Whether expressing an inclination or composing it in a diary, the straightforward demonstration of communicating it enacts a district of the cerebrum engaged with types of discretion and self-guideline. It is a piece like boring an opening in the side of the outrage holder. Leaders sometimes stress that expressing feelings will make them look powerless. It conveys certainty, truth be told. It removes negative energy while furnishing others with a superior comprehension of how a leader ticks.

Extraversion

The amount of Organization Is Too Much? Extraversion mirrors our longing to accompany others and to draw energy from them. Leadership is tied in with affecting individuals, so it very well may be a benefit to be cordial, self-assured, and enthusiastic. There is solid proof that these qualities help executive duties to be seen as leaderlike. The relationship with successful leadership is a lot weaker. You can be excessively self-assured — or excessively fiery. High scores on the extraversion aspect can set off perceptions that the chief is excessively garrulous or overbearing — with the additional ramifications that the individual in question tends not to tune in. Numerous leaders face this challenge, including the country director of a worldwide food varieties goliath we instructed. Examining his proposed action plan, he surrendered: "I've understood that I have a propensity for taking over in gatherings. I need to get better at tuning in and give less emphatic individuals more space to offer their viewpoints. So I want to listen more, however, I additionally need to show I have handled what they've said. The character scores affirm criticism I've received in the past yet not given a lot of consideration to."A straightforward solution for leaders with a propensity to overwhelm procedures is the "four sentences" rule: Anything that you need, as far as possible yourself to four sentences. Then, at that point, inquire: "Do you believe I should continue?" One more feature of extraversion is higher activity levels. This would appear to be a benefit concerning motivating others, however, it can demonstrate wearing. This was a key gaining point for a senior chief from the retail area, who told us: "There's a fine dividing line among fiery and excited — and I likely exceed that limit once in a while. All the while, you wind up making tumult and disconnected telling individuals, instead of animating them." Quick-moving individuals need to remember others' necessities and adjust their energy levels accordingly. In specific, leaders with high energy levels should know that this attitude can make pressure on more slow-paced individuals, particularly those whom the leaders view as sluggish leaning or uncertain. More terrible, these more slow-paced people may then fail to meet expectations, living down to the chief's diminished expectations. As a senior leader from the money area told us: "At whatever point I needed to meet with [one sluggish colleague], he would drain the life out of me. I just attempted to try not to manage him. However, at that point, we were commanded to deal with a similar cross-utilitarian group and I understood that underneath that relaxed outside was an exceptionally sharp brain. I've become substantially more tolerating of his ways due to what he can offer of real value." Or you can be excessively contemplative. Leaders who are all the more inside zeroed in frequently need to figure out how to act like extroverts. A leader who is both saved and serious frequently wears grave looks. They might be given to scowling or tightening their lips. One solution for serious-looking chiefs is to track down an article that prompts them to ponder their look. We recommend they purchase a mug, maybe with a humorous saying on it, to haul around with them. Furthermore, this mug is an update: "What is your demeanor at the present moment?" The thought isn't to grin if you don't feel like it — just to make sure to loosen up your facial muscles.

Unwinding (and grinning) has been displayed to have a physiological effect, on the leader as well as on partners, who will quite often reflect the inclination.

Transparency: The amount of Freshness Is Too Much? Openness incorporates individuals' inclination to show intellectual interest, freedom of judgment, and 10,000-foot view direction. Higher scores on these dimensions have an incentive for leadership roles. But they won't be guaranteed to assist the leader with associating with others. You can be excessively creative or excessively mind-boggling. Estimating on elective perspectives and looking for extra viewpoints can be

baffling for col-associations
who are searching for
clearness, consistency, and
course. Assuming the leader
is effortlessly brought into
"consider the possibility that "
conversations, it tends to be
very disrupted. In the Harvard
Business Audit, Kevin Sharer,
President and presently
administrator of Amgen,
noted: "I'm captivated with
long haul vital other options.
… I like to ponder and discuss
those choices." Yet Sharer
has realized that when a
President frequently examines
conceivable change, "it tends
to undermine the
organization."Leaders with
this trial direction might
require somebody close by
them to keep them grounded.
Sharer has figured out how to
force his discipline: "I've
concluded that I want to take
a gander at these higher
perspective choices a few
times each year and afterward
put them away."Executives
who have a lot of scholarly
interest or innovativeness can
likewise overpower others

with the intricacy or
deliberation of what they are
attempting to convey. They
can wind up befuddling others
as opposed to illuminating
them. They should drive
themselves to work on the
message and to make an
interpretation of their
viewpoints into terms that
others connect with.
Somebody who battled with
an overelaborate belief is
Cristóbal Conde, previous
Chief of Sun-Gard Information
Frameworks. In a New York
Times article, he reviewed a
suggestion he got: "A
supervisor once told me: 'Cris,
you're a brilliant person, yet
that doesn't imply that
individuals can retain a
rundown of 18 activities.
Center around a small bunch
of things.' Exceptionally useful
analysis, and how I've
deciphered that is, the point at
which I do surveyseverything
is threes … three positives
and three things they should
do differently."In addition to
highlighting the critical
objectives, executives inclined

to overcomplicate should adopt a coaching-oriented approach, whereby they check that others follow their meaning and have a chance to contribute. Or you can be too conventional. Leaders at the more conformist end of the spectrum risk coming across as resistant to new ideas. In the words of a chief technology officer we worked with: "I came up through the manufacturing operations. And that suited my temperament. I'm a data guy. I insist on seeing the facts. But now I'm at a [senior] level where people are very willing to share their opinion and expect an opinion. So I've had to teach myself to get out of that conservative zone — and in part, I've done that by volunteering for task forces that give me more of an opportunity to see the big picture."The challenge for executives uncomfortable with ambiguity is to move when not all the information is available. Leaders understanding this tendency in themselves can work to push themselves out of their comfort zone and build up their openness to new experiences.

Agreeableness: How Much Confrontation Is Too Much? Agreeableness is a measure of the importance people place on getting along with others. On the other four dimensions of the Big Five, effective executives typically cluster more on one side of the continuum than the other. With agreeableness, there is no such pattern. The location of the majority varies sharply by national culture, industry, company culture, and even function. To give an extreme example, our coaching work with investment bankers revealed a very low average score on agreeableness. And that is an advantage in an ultra-competitive environment. Executives who score low on agreeableness provide an edge and results focus that is invaluable in business. They are also precious team members, as they are comfortable voicing criticism

and disrupting groupthink.
You can be too rational,
competitive, and watchful.
Executives who are tough-
minded and direct tend to be
unflinching in facing conflict
and tough issues. As a senior
executive from the luxury
goods sector told us: "I'm a
straight talker. I have no
problem telling people that
they messed up — and I'm
always puzzled why people
make such a big deal out of it.
I mean, we're all adults and
we're all trying to improve."
She has a point, but her
failure to comprehend the
discomfort felt by others could
lead them to see her as blunt
or aggressive. For executives
like this, coaching advice
often revolves around the
issue of how the comments
are packaged. The goal is to
make it clear that the critique
relates to the idea, not the
individual submitting it. There
are various ways of softening
criticism. Executives can take
the edge off their remarks by
drawing attention to the
feedback-providing role they

are playing. Using phrases such as "Let me play devil's advocate for a moment" or "If I put on my critic's hat" is one way to accomplish this. If it is hard to find a diplomatic way of saying what needs saying, executives can preface their comments with an acknowledgment that what follows "may seem harsh."Similarly, executives with a strong competitive streak can come across as ruthless, uncooperative, or lacking in the larger perspective. They may get results, but colleagues and subordinates are less likely to trust them. They hence have difficulty building up a strong network; that absence of peer support becomes critical as they reach senior levels. A plant manager in the high-tech sector told us: "When I started as a manager, I was pretty aggressive. I could intimidate people. But that approach will only take you so far. I think I've gone from making my way by trying to be the smartest guy in the room

— constantly picking faults in the arguments of others — to trying more to build on the input of others."Once he realized the discomfort he was creating for those on the receiving end, that executive changed the way he framed his feedback. Rather than laying into the person's flawed logic, he developed a softer touch, explaining that the proposal was perhaps "not yet ready for prime time." He also worked to suppress his tendency to react to ideas with a sentence starting with the word "but." Instead, he tried to begin his responses with "and," which is more inclusive and constructive. It can be helpful for leaders to be politically savvy and sensitive to the dynamics of influence within an organization. But leaders with a low need for agree-ableness can also be too guarded and somewhat defensive, making it difficult for others to trust them. Consider the experience of a project director from the automobile industry: "By nature, I'm not the most open person," he told us. "But I've worked on lots of projects and I've found that unless I share what I'm thinking, it's very difficult to connect with new teams. They're wary. So at the start of a project, I always tell them something about myself, including my family situation, and some of the things I struggle with. I also make a joke about being German. It kick-starts the relationship." Or you can be too considerate.

Conscientiousness:  How Much Focus Is Too Much?

Conscientiousness reflects the extent to which we want to structure and organize our lives. Drive reliability and persistence are important qualities for leaders, but they can prove dysfunctional if they are not properly channeled. You can be too thorough. One risk for highly conscientious leaders is that their perfectionism can cause them to fuss over details while losing sight of the big picture.

That can be a serious problem, as highlighted by the CEO of a family business we worked with. As he put it: "I have quite an appetite for details, so once I get to hear of a problem, I keep asking questions and I have difficulty letting go of it. That can distract me from the essentials. So I'm trying to be more selective about my deep involvement — but it's a work in progress."Executives with this tendency need to ask themselves: "Is this a high-leverage activity — or could my time be better invested elsewhere?" They also need to authorize their direct reports to repeat this question whenever it seems like the executive is getting bogged down in time-wasting details. Perfectionism has another unfortunate consequence. Sensing that their boss is inclined to get too involved or micromanage, employees may grow reluctant to flag issues. Perfectionist executives need to put on their coaching hats and switch to questioning mode so that their input comes across as help, not control. Beyond the professional harm that these preferences can cause, they can also wreak havoc on one's private life. Highly conscientious leaders can become workaholics, obsessive in their pursuit of goals, raising the risk of burnout and poor work-life balance. They can also struggle in situations calling for flexibility. A supply chain director in the telecom sector told us: "I can get overly focused sometimes. I feel an intense responsibility for my area to the extent that I just lose balance — I work too hard, and I neglect my health and my family. And, of course, the less time I spend with my family, the less I feel like I belong with them — and the more I throw myself into the work. So that's a cycle I'm trying to break."An unhealthy commitment to work is not something executives can change overnight. But one approach executives who have this tendency can take is to cut back the working day by 15 minutes. Then, the following week, shave off another 15 minutes, and so on each week until you reach a target workday length.  Or you can make decisions too quickly.

Becoming Self-Aware

Several of the preceding examples suggest ways of managing psychological preferences. The inevitable starting point is self-awareness. Without it, executives will find it hard to evolve or find coping strategies. A survey of 75 members of the Stanford Graduate School of Business Advisory Council rated self-awareness as the most important capability for leaders to develop. Executives need to know where their natural inclinations lie to boost them or compensate for them. Self-awareness is about identifying personal idiosyncrasies — the characteristics that executives take to be the norm but

represent the exception.
Sometimes self-awareness
comes early in one's career,
prompted by a comment from
a trusted colleague or boss. In
an article in Fortune
International, Lauren
Zalaznick, now chairman,
Entertainment & Digital
Networks and Integrated
Media for NBC-Universal,
recalled that the best advice
she ever received was from
her first boss, who told her:
"Throughout your career,
you're going to hear lots of
feedback from show-makers
and peers and employees and
bosses. If you hear a certain
piece of feedback consistently
and you don't agree with it, it
doesn't matter what you think.
Truth is, you're being
perceived that way."
In general, aspiring leaders
need to become aware of
their outlier tendencies and
learn how they are perceived
by others. Passion, hard work,
and intensity are vital traits for
leaders, but those same traits
can also be overwhelming.
The lesson here is

straightforward: The bundle of traits that work for you as a leader right now can become a source of problems on short notice."